Highlights™

Super Challenge
Hidden Pictures®

W9-APK-448

ON THE MOVE

HIGHLIGHTS PRESS
Honesdale, Pennsylvania

Welcome, Hidden Pictures® Puzzlers!

When you finish a puzzle, check it off √. Good luck, and happy puzzling!

Contents

- Half-Pipe Exhibition 4
- Dolphin Watching 5
- Mountain Express 6
- Paper Boats.......................... 7
- Mule's Day Off....................... 8
- Downhill Dash 9
- The Great Skate Race 10
- Life on a Houseboat................ 11
- Family Vacation 12
- In a Tippy Canoe................... 13
- Here We Go! 14
- Building a New Road................ 15
- Soapbox Racers 16–17
- Safe Harbor 18
- Out and About...................... 19
- Baby Emus' Buggy Ride......... 20
- The Snow Queen 21
- Barnstormer......................... 22
- Working on the Railroad.......... 23
- To the Rescue 24
- Next Stop: Piccadilly Circus 25
- Animal Peloton 26–27
- In a Beautiful Balloon 28
- Alien Encounter 29
- The Jet Ski Wins 30
- Steaming through the Tunnel 31
- Everybody, Skate!.............. 32–33
- Blast Off! 34
- Ice Sailing 35
- Bridge Builders.............. 36–37
- Streets of San Francisco 38
- Seaworthy Sneaker................. 39
- Taking a Break...................... 40
- Oops!................................ 41
- Jumping Jalopy 42
- Tugboat Ted......................... 43
- A Great Escape 44–45
- Switch Stance...................... 46
- Big-Wheel Bikes 47
- Earth Movers 48–49
- Ready for Takeoff 50–51
- Skate Date 52
- Into the Wind 53
- The Cats Pull Ahead.......... 54–55
- Surfside Fun 56
- Downhill Run........................ 57
- Eddie's Scooter 58
- Down at the Dock.................. 59
- Space Explorer..................... 60
- Two for the Road................... 61
- At the Diner 62
- Coming In for a Landing.......... 63
- Gator Gets Air...................... 64
- Cherry Picker to the Rescue..... 65
- Whitewater Turtles................. 66
- Leopard in Flight 67
- Across the Channel........... 68–69
- Rodent Road Race 70
- Railroad Crossing...................71
- But Will It Fly? 72

Cover Illustration by Charles Jordan

Land, Ho! 73

Sunday in the Park 74

On the Road 75

Jolly Trolley.......................... 76

Fireboat Drill 77

Ski School 78

On the Riverboat.................... 79

At the Lake 80

Skydiving Skunks 81

They're Off!.......................... 82

Zero Gravity......................... 83

Friends on the River 84–85

The Last Turn 86

Ahoy There! 87

Coming Through 88

Flight School........................ 89

Wild Ride 90

Steep Grade 91

Touring the Everglades 92–93

Moose on the Loose 94

Space Surfing 95

Floating Down the River 96–97

Rat Race 98

Boarding the School Bus......... 99

Pelican on Waterskis............. 100

Scenic Flight........................ 101

Cross-Country Sighting 102

On a High-Wheeler 103

Tour Bus Down Under 104

Yacht Race 105

Breakdown on the Bridge 106

Gondolas on the Canal 107

Lift to the Top...................... 108

Test Flight 109

Race to the Bottom.......... 110–111

Return from the Sea.............. 112

Long-Distance Ride 113

A Drive in the Country 114

Fisherman's Cove................. 115

Bunny on a Bike................... 116

Ahead of the Clouds 117

Slippery Slope..................... 118

Crop Duster 119

Heavy Equipment........... 120–121

Special Purchase 122–123

Bon Voyage 124

Freeriding Downhill 125

Air Show 126–127

Loads of Logs 128–129

Through the Golden Gate 130

Answers 131

Half-Pipe Exhibition

crescent moon, handbell, drinking straw, ring, golf club, screwdriver, magnifying glass, fish, paintbrush, mushroom, mallet, hat, heart, spoon, pennant, ladder, candle, teacup, cupcake, pencil, funnel, tweezers, needle

Dolphin Watching

ice-cream bar, frying pan, glove, ring, teapot, key, egg, flyswatter, telescope, toothbrush, dragonfly, parrot, rabbit

Illustrated by Valeri Gorbachev

ntain Express

unicorn, cactus, baseball cap, candy cane, camera, teacup, comb, cupcake, carrot, piece of candy, caterpillar, can of paint

Paper Boats

baseball bat, handbell, toothbrush, candle, canoe, celery, teacup, cupcake, fish, flashlight, hat, musical note, slice of pie, swan, trowel

Illustrated by Linda Weller

Mule's Day Off

Downhill Dash

slice of pie, bell, ice-cream cone, toothbrush, slice of cake, scrub brush, pencil, pushpin, crayon, artist's brush, fishhook, acorn

Illustrated by Charles Jordan

The Great Skate Race

tack, fire hydrant, bell, clothespin, crescent moon, star, ax, horseshoe, mushroom, light bulb, teacup, lamp, dragonfly

Life on a Houseboat

archer's bow, baseball cap, glove, mug, pie, open book, bowl, crayon, hat, light bulb, pickax, snake

Illustrated by Kit Wray

Family Vacation

heart, dog, seal, star, ruler, glove, clock, sailboat, eyeglasses, toothbrush, saw, magnifying glass, teacup, sock

Illustrated by Tim Davis

In a Tippy Canoe

duck, closed umbrella, light bulb, cup, mallet, fishhook, ring, toothbrush, pencil, pail, plunger, fork, penguin

Illustrated by Valeri Gorbachev

Here We Go!

boomerang, coat hanger, crescent moon, hammer, 2 hearts, key, glove, bat, butterfly, comb, fishhook, high-heeled shoe, light bulb, pickax, sock

Illustrated by Arieh Zeldich

Building a New Road

pen, artist's brush, golf club, crayon, toothbrush, whistle, mallet, spoon, key, magnifying glass, mitten, shoe

Illustrated by Charles Jordan

Soapbox Racers

GO MOUSE!

Illustrated by Charles Jordan

Safe Harbor

flag, crescent moon, pen, horseshoe, fishhook, ladder, hockey stick, pitchfork, nail, comb, domino, pickax, dolphin, spool of thread, coat hanger, baseball bat, shoe, button

Illustrated by Arieh Zeldich

Out and About

candle, glove, roller skate, hammer, pencil, slice of cake, top hat, sailboat, rabbit, open book, saw, teapot, butter knife

Illustrated by Holly Carryer

Baby Emus' Buggy Ride

rabbit, carrot, frog, fish, light bulb, candle, magnifying glass, boomerang, comb, lizard, anchor, mouse, pitcher, flashlight

The Snow Queen

cane, plunger, closed umbrella, ice-cream bar, ice-cream cone, bell, key, slice of orange, ring, crown, domino, spool of thread, fishhook

Illustrated by Arieh Zeldich

Barnstormer

shoe, bell, hoe, safety pin, pushpin, apple half, mitten, cupcake, book, comb, feather, trowel, paintbrush, radish, pencil, pliers

Working on the Railroad

3 books, boot, bowl, chicken, crescent moon, eyeglasses, flashlight, goblet, hammer, horseshoe, nail, spoon

Illustrated by Kit Wray

To the Rescue

Illustrated by R. Michael Palan

Next Stop: Piccadilly Circus

wristwatch, artist's brush, hammer, high-heeled boot, bell, hockey stick, safety pin, star, bird, suitcase, telescope, present, compass, feather, hat, canoe

Illustrated by Jeri Simkus

Animal Peloton

apple core, arrow, handbell, boot, broom, clothespin, comb, duck, dustpan, fork, hammer,
ice-cream cone, insect, iron, mouse, paper clip, pencil, roller skate, sailboat, saw, shark, shovel,

spoon, suitcase, teddy bear, telephone, tube of toothpaste, bird, turtle

Illustrated by Valeri Gorbachev

In a Beautiful Balloon

rabbit, flute, monkey, bird, bucket, flower, toy top, umbrella, boot, sailboat, open book, rooster's head, letter *H*

Illustrated by Jeri Simkus

Alien Encounter

ice pop, ice-cream soda, nail, ring, hammer, tack, duck, slice of pie, light bulb, wristwatch, shoe, whale, cupcake

Illustrated by R. Michael Palan

The Jet Ski Wins

ring, domino, golf club, pennant, fishhook, coat hanger, 2 hearts, hockey stick, boomerang, key, football, plunger, camera, light bulb, ladder

Illustrated by Arieh Zeldich

Steaming through the Tunnel

book, eyeglasses, toothbrush, chicken's head, hat, battery, mallet, heart, scissors, necklace, bat, paper clip, glove, airplane

Illustrated by Tim Davis

Everybody, Skate!

Blast Off!

baseball bat, handbell, pennant, fork, heart, ice-cream cone, key, knife, nail, needle, ring, shoe, snake, toothbrush, wishbone, worm

Ice Sailing

crochet hook, baseball bat, slice of cake, heart, nail, mitten, mushroom, safety pin, pennant, butter knife, paddle, pencil, golf club, carrot

Bridge Builders

sock, comb, open book, envelope, boomerang, golf club, paintbrush, saw, fish, tack, spool of thread, pencil

Illustrated by R. Michael Palan

Streets of San Francisco

ladder, bird, ruler, teacup, shoe, telescope, golf club, woman's head, eyeglasses, sailboat, horse's head, artist's brush, pencil, piglet in a basket, elf's hat

Seaworthy Sneaker

telephone receiver, iron, dragonfly, saw, bow, spoon, pennant, mug, high-heeled shoe, chick, key, elf's hat, caterpillar, paper clip

Illustrated by Valeri Gorbachev

Taking a Break

artist's brush, mallet, musical note, pencil, crayon, book, crown, magnifying glass, hoe, golf club, eyeglasses, flashlight

Illustrated by Charles Jordan

Oops!

tepee, mushroom, teacup, flower, heart, bell, snake, wishbone, needle, ruler, yo-yo, olive, spoon, ring

Illustrated by Diana Zourelias

Jumping Jalopy

boomerang, elephant's head, bird, heart, ice-cream cone, strawberry, magnifying glass, snail, pickax, hat, fish, toothbrush, key, pair of pants, ring

Illustrated by Tim Davis

Tugboat Ted

apple, ax, balloon, bird, heart, mop, mushroom, pencil, slice of pie, screwdriver, snake, toy top, watermelon

Illustrated by George Wildman

A Great Escape

key, snake, ring, ice-cream cone, slice of bread, spoon, drinking straw, slice of pie,
comb, candle, canoe, wishbone, teacup, glove, nail, hairbrush, lollipop, bottle, letter,

fish, toothbrush, fork, alligator, saw

Switch Stance

Illustrated by Tim Davis

46

Big-Wheel Bikes

banana, bell, boot, feather, fish, fork, frog, glove, moth, slice of pie, ring, spoon, turtle

Illustrated by Ron Leiser

Earth Movers

ruler, drill, lunchbox, mallet, nail, screwdriver, pencil, shovel, saw, screw, boot, trowel

Ready for Takeoff

hoe, shovel, frying pan, pushpin, golf club, mug, pen, bell, feather, mallet, artist's brush, nail, shoe, pencil, ice-cream cone, hairbrush, slice of pie, crayon, mushroom, spatula,

Illustrated by Charles Jordan

Skate Date

Into the Wind

spoon, feather, snail, frog, broom, swan, envelope, comb, baseball cap, toucan's head, bird, pennant, crayon, kite

Illustrated by Kit Wray

The Cats Pull Ahead

spatula, feather, hoe, pencil, dustpan, mitten, ring, flag, carrot, slice of pizza, hairbrush, banana, slice of cake, mug, sailboat, candle, nail, safety pin, artist's brush, pushpin, tube of toothpaste,

slice of pie, handbag, sock, book, golf club, bicycle pump

Surfside Fun

Illustrated by George Wildman

56

Downhill Run

teacup, golf club, ice-cream cone, artist's brush, nail, pen, dessert dish, bell, book, pencil, ring, slice of cake

Illustrated by Charles Jordan

Eddie's Scooter

toothbrush, pen, slice of pie, key, funnel, paintbrush, teacup, pencil, wedge of apple, ladle, shoe, tack

Down at the Dock

wishbone, coffeepot, toothbrush, iron, saucepan, screwdriver, paintbrush, crayon, carrot, sock, envelope, slice of pie, safety pin

Illustrated by Leslie Franz

Space Explorer

banana, bell, sailboat, light bulb, candle, crown, teacup, fish, frog, heart, ice-cream cone, ring, saw, spoon, toothbrush

Illustrated by Tim Davis

Two for the Road

dog, moon, pencil, teacup, spoon, boot, screwdriver, hammer, mitten, snake, needle, toothbrush

Illustrated by R. Michael Palan

At the Diner

hatchet, slice of pizza, needle, elf's hat, ring, pencil, top hat, apple, pennant, bag of popcorn, crescent moon, teacup, golf club, slice of cake, banana, drinking straw, ice-cream cone

Illustrated by R. Michael Palan

Coming In for a Landing

candle, book, ice-cream bar, pennant, ring, slice of cake, bicycle pump, turnip, fishhook, pushpin, saucepan, tack

Illustrated by Charles Jordan

Gator Gets Air

Illustrated by Rocky Fuller

Cherry Picker to the Rescue

mallet, wishbone, funnel, book, ring, candle, mushroom, screwdriver, carrot, safety pin, fishhook, ice-cream cone

Illustrated by Charles Jordan

Whitewater Turtles

teacup, spoon, letter, crescent moon, musical note, fishhook, mitten, apple, high-heeled shoe, duck, needle, nail, artist's brush, mushroom, wishbone, crayon, fork, crown

Illustrated by Mike DeSantis

Leopard in Flight

screw, comb, stork, fishhook, octopus, spoon, bow, heart, ice-cream cone, cowboy hat, party hat, handbell, in-line skate

Illustrated by Valeri Gorbachev

Across the Channel

Rodent Road Race

chicken, scissors, horn, owl, light bulb, hairbrush, padlock, handbell, arrow, carrot, pumpkin, cat, bird, vase

Illustrated by Valeri Gorbachev

70

Railroad Crossing

sock, elephant's head, artist's brush, rolling pin, teapot, oil can, king's head, ice-cream cone, fish, carrot, nail, fork, dog's head, scissors, kite, toothbrush, bowl

Illustrated by Ralph Owen

But Will It Fly?

egg, bowl, flag, book, belt, light bulb, mop, doughnut, goblet, nail, tack, teacup, baseball, insect

Land, Ho!

bat, crown, comb, hammer, heart, ice-cream cone, mouse, nail, open book, pencil, saw, shark, teacup, toothbrush

Illustrated by Tim Davis

Sunday in the Park

apple core, carrot, slice of cake, yo-yo, bell, magic wand, key, candle, nail, pushpin, mushroom, safety pin, slice of pie

Illustrated by Charles Jordan

On the Road

toothbrush, rabbit, pizza, weasel, pencil, book, hamster's head, crescent moon, spoon, cardinal's head, hot dog, mouse

Illustrated by Kit Wray

Jolly Trolley

baby's bottle, boomerang, candle, crescent moon, eyeglasses, golf club, pizza, book, butterfly, four-leaf clover, fried egg, fishing pole, harmonica, spoon

Illustrated by Kathy Goetzel

Fireboat Drill

domino, ladder, safety pin, coat hanger, paper clip, shovel, fishhook, boomerang, pushpin, paddle, ring, hockey stick, slice of orange, button, ice-cream bar, tennis ball, eyeglasses

Ski School

bird, teacup, coat hanger, mouse, paper clip, in-line skate, spoon, ant, brush, pennant, needle, pencil, turtle, ice-cream cone

Illustrated by Valeri Gorbachev

On the Riverboat

spool of thread, wedge of cheese, bottle, dog, saw, comb, slice of orange, ladder, bird, banjo, toothbrush, fish, cooking pot

Illustrated by Georgina Hargreaves

At the Lake

arrow, lizard, broom, teapot, archer's bow, cane, whistle, kite, penguin, fish, bird, dog, paper clip

BOATS FOR HIRE

Illustrated by Mij Colson-Barnum

Skydiving Skunks

hoe, needle, book, funnel, envelope, mushroom, lightning bolt, bell, football, ring, fish, saw, peanut, toothbrush

Illustrated by Rocky Fuller

They're Off!

Illustrated by Charles Jordan

Zero Gravity

telescope, wrench, slipper, envelope, 2 toothbrushes, ring, light bulb, bell, hat, spool of thread, ice-cream bar, teacup, hot dog, scissors

Illustrated by R. Michael Palan

Friends on the River

sneaker, banana, flashlight, glove, lollipop, candle, funnel, teacup, frying pan, broom, spoon, flag

The Last Turn

banana, crown, eyeglasses, fish, handbell, hat, ice-cream cone, kite, paper clip, ring, snake, straight pin, toothbrush

Ahoy There!

Illustrated by Diana Zourelias

Coming Through

slice of pie, flag, needle, open book, snake, lollipop, bell, candle, toothbrush, crescent moon, oil drum, ladder, dog bowl

Illustrated by George Wildman

Flight School

Illustrated by Charles Jordan

Wild Ride

fork, fish, bird, spoon, heart, crescent moon, duck, nail, hatchet, comb, snake, mouse, elf's hat

Illustrated by Kit Wray

Steep Grade

ice-cream cone, spatula, mallet, spool of thread, bell, feather, pen, pencil, banana, slice of cake, safety pin, mushroom

Illustrated by Charles Jordan

Touring the Everglades

Moose on the Loose

arrow, handbell, bird, dog, duck, fork, hairbrush, iron, key, spoon, nail, pennant, shoe, teacup

Illustrated by Valeri Gorbachev

Space Surfing

banana, cactus, fish, flashlight, ghost, ladle, crescent moon, needle, ring, sock, trowel, tube of toothpaste, wishbone, worm

Illustrated by R. Michael Palan

Floating Down the River

fried egg, candy cane, handbag, penguin, pennant, banana, baby seal, bat, heart, pencil, pumpkin, flashlight

Illustrated by Diana Zourelias

Rat Race

slice of watermelon, candy cane, arrow, fishhook, hamburger, spool of thread, needle, pencil, candle, pennant, tack, slice of pie, drinking glass, telescope

Illustrated by Rocky Fuller

Boarding the School Bus

feather, celery, slice of pie, pushpin, radish, ice-cream cone, bicycle pump, ladder, slice of cake, ring, toothbrush, golf club

Illustrated by Charles Jordan

Pelican on Waterskis

boot, crescent moon, fishhook, golf club, hatchet, heart, hedgehog, straight pin, open book, oyster shell, pineapple, ring, scissors

Scenic Flight

shovel, duck, mug, boot, rabbit, sailboat, crescent moon, needle, worm, tweezers, mitten, lollipop

Illustrated by Kit Wray

Cross-Country Sighting

Illustrated by Katharine Dodge

102

On a High-Wheeler

Illustrated by Judy Freidel

Tour Bus Down Under

boomerang, 2 bananas, nail, apple, sock, fork, parrot, mitten, fan, 3 mice, pencil, spoon

Illustrated by Valeri Gorbachev

Yacht Race

bat, candle, ghost, top hat, ice-cream cone, ice-cream bar, mitten, needle, pencil, pennant, sock, pointy hat

Illustrated by Janet Robertson

Breakdown on the Bridge

shoe, bell, mitten, fish, shovel, ice-cream cone, pencil, croquet mallet, screw, tube of toothpaste, key, magnifying glass

Illustrated by Charles Jordan

Gondolas on the Canal

slice of pizza, wishbone, hatchet, duck, shark, pointy hat, shoe, crayon, bottle, toothbrush, knitted hat, pennant

Illustrated by Kit Wray

Lift to the Top

butterfly, cherry, crescent moon, egg, fishhook, flag, fork, ladle, lollipop, open book, pencil, shark, tack, teacup, tennis ball, worm

Illustrated by Arieh Zeldich

Test Flight

flashlight, loaf of bread, hammer, bird, binoculars, letter C, nail, kite, pitcher, clarinet, violin bow, cat's head, hockey stick, hat

Illustrated by Elizabeth Allyn Hendricks

Race to the Bottom

apple core, artist's brush, banana, bell, book, butterfly, carrot, dustpan, flashlight, flower, golf club, needle, paintbrush, pencil, pushpin, ring, shovel, slice of bread, slice of cake,

spoon, teacup, tube of toothpaste, vase, candle

Return from the Sea

bird, stork, 2 kangaroos, iron, key, 2 cats, bell, guitar, rabbit, teacup, sock, belt, sea gull

Illustrated by Valeri Gorbachev

Long-Distance Ride

safety pin, closed umbrella, pushpin, mug, candle, artist's brush, spatula, shovel, mitten, feather, nail, pencil

Illustrated by Charles Jordan

A Drive in the Country

Illustrated by Valeri Gorbachev

Fisherman's Cove

walnut, seal, rabbit, ear of corn, pointy hat, jar, goat's head, purse, dog, totem pole, anchor, table, kite, grapes, fish

Illustrated by Jeri Simkus

Bunny on a Bike

butterfly, slice of cake, candle, carrot, cupcake, ice-cream cone, musical note, pencil, pushpin, screwdriver, spoon, tack

Ahead of the Clouds

celery, hamster, walnut, pencil, anchor, feather, eagle's head, dolphin, sock, telescope, fish, slice of bread, sea horse

Illustrated by Mij Colson-Barnum

Slippery Slope

glove, hockey stick, swan, cat, pie, spoon, hot dog, bird, clover, elf's head, light bulb, rabbit, turtle, lamb's head, elf's hat, heart

Illustrated by Mij Colson-Barnum

Crop Duster

ladder, hoe, golf club, kite, artist's brush, rake, ice-cream cone, stamp, slice of pizza, flag, open book, boot, ring, snake, slice of pie, needle, muffin pan

Illustrated by Millard Hall

Heavy Equipment

bicycle pump, crayon, snow shovel, grapes, screwdriver, funnel, briefcase, chair, owl, boot, flowerpot, apple half, artist's brush, slice of cake with a candle, magnifying glass, ice-cream,

coat hanger, canoe, flashlight, open book, safety pin, slice of pie, pointy hat, telephone, cowboy hat, flower, goblet

Illustrated by Charles Jordan

Special Purchase

ladder, goblet, toothbrush, paper airplane, handbell, book, eyeglasses, broom, heart, domino, envelope, yo-yo, ax, golf club, spatula, golf ball, horseshoe, ring, hockey stick, flag, button,

cube, paintbrush, candle, turtle, candy cane, comb, boot, drinking glass, pennant

Bon Voyage

crescent moon, heart, handbell, ladder, spatula, paper clip, envelope, toothbrush, boot, hockey stick, magnet, trowel, boomerang

Illustrated by Arieh Zeldich

Freeriding Downhill

artist's brush, comb, crescent moon, crown, teacup, ice-cream cone, ice-cream bar, mitten, nail, sock, slice of pie, toothbrush, toothpaste

Illustrated by R. Michael Palan

Air Show

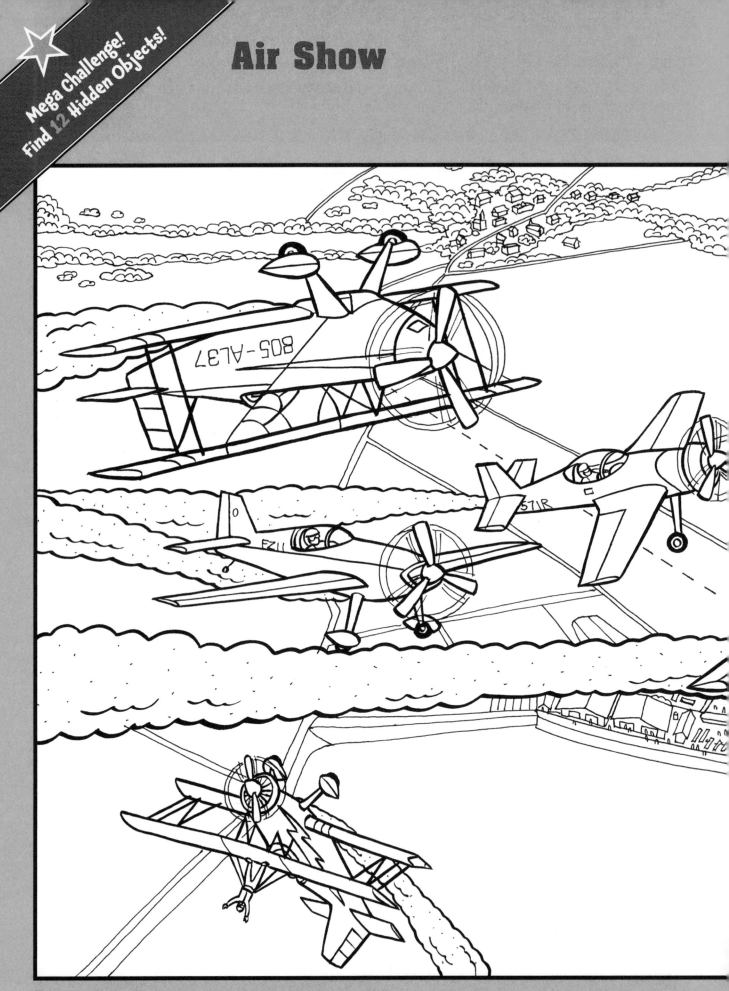

C-GAK7

5

Illustrated by Tim Davis

Loads of Logs

golf club, artist's brush, feather, ice-cream bar, kite, pen, hoe, shovel, slice of pie, carrot, nail, closed umbrella, frying pan, funnel, crayon, slice of cake, safety pin, spatula, mug, pencil,

pliers, candle, mitten, spoon, pushpin, ring, open book

Through the Golden Gate

fish, hammer, mouse, dolphin, mug, seashell, fork, butterfly, pencil, feather, sea gull, leaf, electrical outlet

Illustrated by Glen Dines

Answers

▼ Page 4

▼ Page 5

▼ Page 6

▼ Page 7

▼ Page 8

▼ Page 9

▼ Page 10

▼ Page 11

▼ Page 12

Answers

▼Page 13

▼Page 14

▼Page 15

▼Pages 16–17

▼Page 18

▼Page 19

▼Page 20

▼Page 21

Answers

▼Page 22

▼Page 23

▼Page 24

▼Page 25

▼Pages 26–27

▼Page 28

▼Page 29

▼Page 30

Answers

▼Page 31

▼Pages 32–33

▼Page 34

▼Page 35

▼Pages 36–37

▼Page 38

Answers

▼Page 39

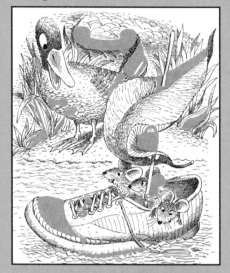

▼Page 40

▼Page 41

▼Page 42

▼Page 43

▼Pages 44–45

▼Page 46

Answers

▼ Page 47

▼ Pages 48–49

▼ Pages 50–51

▼ Page 52

▼ Page 53

▼ Pages 54–55

Answers

▼ Page 56

▼ Page 57

▼ Page 58

▼ Page 59

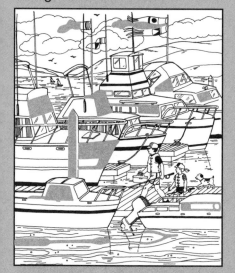

▼ Page 60

▼ Page 61

▼ Page 62

▼ Page 63

▼ Page 64

Answers

▼Page 65

▼Page 66

▼Page 67

▼Pages 68–69

▼Page 70

▼Page 71

▼Page 72

▼Page 73

▼ Page 74

▼ Page 75

▼ Page 76

▼ Page 77

▼ Page 78

▼ Page 79

▼ Page 80

▼ Page 81

▼ Page 82

Answers

▼ Page 83

▼ Pages 84–85

▼ Page 86

▼ Page 87

▼ Page 88

▼ Page 89

▼ Page 90

▼ Page 91

Answers

▼Pages 92–93

▼Page 94

▼Page 95

▼Pages 96–97

▼Page 98

▼Page 99

▼Page 100

Answers

▼Page 101

▼Page 102

▼Page 103

▼Page 104

▼Page 105

▼Page 106

▼Page 107

▼Page 108

▼Page 109

Answers

▼ Pages 110–111

▼ Page 112

▼ Page 113

▼ Page 114

▼ Page 115

▼ Page 116

▼ Page 117

▼ Page 118

143

Answers

▼ Page 119

▼ Pages 120–121

▼ Pages 122–123

▼ Page 124

▼ Page 125

▼ Pages 126–127